ADVENTURES IN THE GREAT OUTDOORS

FISHING

ROBYN HARDYMAN

WINDMILL BOOKS
New York

Published in 2014 by Windmill Books, An Imprint of Rosen Publishing
29 East 21st Street, New York, NY 10010

Produced for Windmill by Calcium Creative Ltd
Editor for Calcium Creative Ltd: Sarah Eason
US Editor: Sara Howell
Designer: Emma DeBanks

Photo credits: Cover: Dreamstime: Monkey Business Images. Inside: Shutterstock: Alexnika
4, Arena Creative 14b, Auremar 8, CCat82 25, Norman Chan 13l, Deepspacedave 26m,
Goodluz 1, 19, Gorillaimages 18, Sergey Goruppa 26b, Rob Hainer 26t, Imageman 15,
Kaczor58 14t, Kletr 10, Kzww 12, Petr Malyshev 13r, Michaeljung 16, Monkey Business
Images 5, Susan Montgomery 7, Paul B. Moore 6, Mountainpix 23, Oliveromg 9,
Pinponpix 17, Regina Pryanichnikova 20, Heather Renee 21, Galushko Sergey 11,
Bjorn Stefanson 29, Steven Russell Smith Photos 27b, Tab62 22, Cappi Thompson 28,
Dan Thornberg 27t, Txking 24.

Library of Congress Cataloging-in-Publication Data

Hardyman, Robyn.
Fishing / by Robyn Hardyman.
pages cm. — (Adventures in the great outdoors)
Includes index.
ISBN 978-1-61533-749-1 (library binding) — ISBN 978-1-61533-815-3 (pbk.) —
ISBN 978-1-61533-816-0 (6-pack)
1. Fishing—Juvenile literature. I. Title.
SH445.H37 2014
799.1—dc23
2013004076
Manufactured in the United States of America

CPSIA Compliance Information: Batch #BS13WM: For Further Information contact Windmill Books, New York, New York at 1-866-478-0556

Contents

Fishing

People have been fishing for tens of thousands of years to catch food to eat. The sport of fishing with a **rod**, line, and hook is called **angling**. It's different from fishing with large nets to catch fish for food. Angling is popular all over the world, because it's a wonderful way to connect with nature and enjoy an adventure in the great outdoors.

There are three kinds of angling. The first is sea fishing, when you catch saltwater fish from a boat or the shore. The second is game fishing. This is catching salmon or trout. The third kind is coarse fishing. This is catching other **freshwater** fish and it's the most popular fishing sport today. This book tells you all about this kind of fishing.

There's nothing quite like the satisfaction of catching a fish!

STAY SAFE!

Deep water can be dangerous. Always fish with an adult and be careful near water.

Adult anglers will be happy to pass their fishing knowledge and experience on to you.

You can go fishing at any age. You just need some basic equipment, a love of being outdoors, and plenty of patience. You may have to wait a while for a fish to bite, but it's worth the wait when you feel a tug on the line and you **reel** in your catch. It feels great when you **land** your own fish! If you get hooked by fishing, you could even join a local club. Clubs hold competitions and you will get to talk to other anglers about your favorite sport, too.

Plan Your Trip

To make the most of your fishing trip, you need to do a little planning before you go. There is a lot to think about and some important questions to ask before your trip.

One of the most important questions to ask is whether you need a **license** to fish. Most states don't require kids to have a license, but the adult you're with will need one. You can buy a fishing license at your **tackle** store or state fish and wildlife office. You'll find the local fishing regulations there, too.

It's important to know fishing regulations and to follow the rules. Fishing isn't allowed at certain times of year, because the fish are laying their eggs. Preventing fishing at these times means the supply of fish is protected for the future. You may also need permission from the landowner or local fishing club to fish in your chosen location.

Don't forget to take something to sit on and the right clothing for the weather, including a hat to protect you from the Sun or the rain.

Fishing Log Book

Make a fishing log to record your successes.

Explore This!

You will need:
- hardcover notebook
- camera
- portable weighing scale

1 Decide the type of information you want to record, such as the date and time of the trip, location, weather, and who you're fishing with.

2 Decide what you want to record about your catch, such as species of fish and its weight.

3 Plan out how you want to write the information in your log book.

4 Pack a camera to take photos of your fish.

5 Take a portable weighing scale to weigh your catch.

CATCH AND RELEASE

SELECTIVE RELEASE
RECYCLE THE BIG ONES

STAY SAFE! Remember to take a first aid kit to fix any cuts and scrapes.

Remember to follow the signs wherever you are fishing.

Get the Gear

You can't catch fish without some essential equipment, or tackle. The most essential pieces of equipment are the fishing rod and reel.

There are different rods for catching different types of fish. Start with a general purpose rod, around 5 feet (1.5 m) long. It should be light enough to be comfortable for you to hold. This type of rod has sections, which you fit together and line up.

The **spool** that holds the line faces toward the rod's tip.

A lever called the **bale arm** holds the line on the reel.

The reel is for holding the line and wheeling it in and out of the water.

Reel and Line

This is how to attach the reel and line to your rod.

You will need:
- rod
- reel
- fishing line

1 Slide the reel fittings on the rod over the foot of the reel.

2 Hold out the rod with the reel on the underside, facing the ground. Open the bale arm on the reel.

3 Unwind around 3 feet (1 m) of line and tie one end to the reel's spool with a knot. Wrap it around a few times, then close the bale arm.

4 Turn the handle of the reel away from you. This makes the bale arm spin and the line slide onto the spool.

5 Stop turning when the line has filled up the spool. Cut the line.

6 Turn the reel handle toward you to unwind the line. Thread the end of the line through the rings along the length of the rod.

A spinning reel is suitable for all types and sizes of fish.

9

Hooks and Knots

It's the hook at the end of the line that catches hold of the fish's mouth. To catch different fish, you'll need to know what types of hook to use and how to tie them onto your line.

Remember to match the size of the hook to the size of the fish you're likely to catch. If the hook is too small, the fish could swallow it. If a fish does swallow a hook, you can remove it with a special hook-removal tool. If the hook is too big, the fish won't bite.

One end of the hook has a small eye. This is where you tie the hook to your line. To do this, you'll need to know how to tie fishing knots. The fishing line is a thin, see-through wire. When tying any knot, always wet the line with water to make it slippery.

STAY SAFE!

Hooks are sharp! Handle them with care and always hold the line above the hook if possible.

*Some fish hooks have a **barb** on them. This is difficult to remove from a fish's mouth, so always use hooks without barbs.*

Knotty Business

Learn to tie a **cinch knot**, which is perfect for tying the hook to the line.

You will need:
- hook
- some line

1 Pass the line through the hook's eye twice, making a large loop.

2 Wrap the end of the line around the main line four or five times.

3 Now pass the free end of the line through the big double loop near the eye end of the line.

4 Wet the line and pull the end tight to close the knot.

*A hook and a **fly** are attached by a knot to this fishing line.*

Fish Bait

To catch fish, you need to tempt them with something good to eat! This is the bait. Choosing the right bait is one of the main skills of fishing.

Live fish eat live food, so it's easy to see why they prefer live bait. Live bait includes worms, grubs, and insects. The downside of using live bait is that you have to keep the bait alive. Grubs, for example, last only around one week if you keep them cool. However, you can use food such as pieces of cheese, small balls of bread, and corn instead of live bait.

Anglers often use artificial bait instead of live bait. Flies are made from feathers, fur, and wire, so they look like insects. **Lures** are made from wood, plastic, or metal, to look like small fish. Both flies and lures have a hook.

Fishing flies such as these are designed to look like insects.

Worms for Bait

Explore This!

Find worms and attach them correctly onto your line.

You will need:
- small implement for digging, such as a trowel
- small plastic box with a lid
- hook

1 On the riverbank, dig in a patch of soil to find some worms.

2 Put some soil in the plastic box and store your worms inside it.

3 Attach a worm to your hook by pushing the hook all the way through its body.

4 Push the hook through the middle of the worm. That way, the worm will wriggle at both ends.

Light-colored lures are best for bright, clear water.

You can even use candy such as jellybeans for bait!

Bobbers and Sinkers

In some fishing situations, you'll want to use either a bobber or a sinker on your line, as well as the bait.

Bobbers are used when you're trying to catch fish near the surface of the water. Bobbers are round or oblong shapes made of plastic and are attached to the line above the hook and bait. They float on the surface. When bobbers move or disappear, it's a sign that you've got a bite! Bobbers are great for shallow, calm water.

Sinkers do the opposite job of bobbers. They're heavy and are used to catch fish near the bottom of the water. Sinkers are threaded onto the line and drag it down. They come in different shapes for use in different types of water.

The hook with the bait is way down in the water, below the bobber.

*Use a **tackle box** to keep your kit organized. There are lots of compartments for keeping bobbers, sinkers, hooks, bait, and line.*

14

Setting Up the Bobber

Get your bobber set up just right on the line.

You will need:
- line, hook, and bait
- bobber and bobber ring
- split shot

1 Slide the bobber ring onto the line around 3 feet (1 m) from the end and push the bright end of the bobber through the ring.

2 Thread the line through the eye at the other end of the bobber.

3 Attach the hook and bait to the end of the line.

4 Squeeze three **split shot** onto the line, a few inches (cm) apart.

5 **Cast** the line into the water. Only the top of the bobber should be visible on the surface.

Split shot are small weights that hold down the hook and make the bobber sit upright.

STAY SAFE! Don't use bobbers if ducks or swans are on the water. They will go for the bait and get caught on the hook.

15

The Perfect Cast

You're all set and ready to choose the perfect place to cast your line. Now, where are the fish?

You'll need to do a little detective work to find fish. Look for clues such as bubbles or ripples in the water. Undisturbed areas, below overhanging trees or in weeds, are often good places to find fish. Avoid anywhere many boats pass by because they are likely to disturb the fish.

You can cast, or throw your line, underarm or overhead. Either way, it's all about timing and releasing the line at exactly the right moment to make sure you put the bait where you want it without making a big splash. Underarm casting is best if there are trees, bushes, or power cables around you.

If you use overhead casting your bait will travel farther.

Overhead Casting

Here's how to master an overhead cast.

1 In one hand, hold the rod almost upright.

2 Turn the handle to wind in the line until it hangs a third of the way down the rod.

3 With your finger, press the line coming off the reel up against the rod handle. Then open the bale arm.

4 Swing the rod back a little, then quickly push away with your top hand and pull down with your bottom hand.

5 Straighten your top arm, then take your finger off the line. The line will fly forward into the water.

STAY SAFE!

Don't cast from slippery places, such as rocks. Stay at least 100 yards (91 m) from overhead power cables.

It takes a little practice to master overhead casting.

17

You've Got a Bite!

You feel a pull on the line, and you've got a bite! Now you need to get your fish out of the water before it escapes. If it's a good size, it will try to swim away. The trick is to let the fish get tired, so it will be easier to land. This is known as "playing the fish."

To play the fish, set the hook firmly in the fish's mouth. This is called the **strike**. Reel in any slack line and sharply raise the tip of your rod. A big fish, struggling hard, will break the line and get away, so let out some line.

The rod tip will bend as the fish swims away from you. As it swims back toward you, lift the rod tip up to tighten the line and reel it in slowly. Do this several times. Each time, you are bringing the fish closer to the bank and tiring it. Be patient, the fish is almost yours!

You may need some help to reel in a big fish!

STAY
SAFE!

Make sure you are standing on firm ground as you play a fish. A big fish pulling hard on the line could pull you into the water if you're on slippery rocks.

Keep a close watch on your fish as you bring it in.

You need to act fast when you're going for the strike. This is especially true in summer, when the fish are more active. In winter, they may not move toward the bait so quickly. Then you may have to wait a few seconds more. You will learn from experience. When the fish get away with your bait, you'll see how fast you have to be!

19

Land It!

Landing your fish is the most exciting part of any fishing trip. It's really important not to give up now. Remember to use the right landing techniques to make sure you get your fish!

By now you should have played the fish until it is tired and close to the bank. Lower the end of your rod to keep the fish under the water. Bring it to the edge by turning the reel handle away from you to shorten the line. Now lift the rod tip upward again. You'll need another person to hold the landing net. That person should slide the net under the fish as you hold up the rod tip to keep the line tight. Gradually tighten the line further, while the other person lifts the net out of the water.

Have your landing net ready to take the fish as you land it.

It's a proud moment when a fish is finally yours.

If you are landing a small fish, you can just bring it in toward the bank. Now lift the tip of your rod until you see the fish come out of the water. With one hand, hold the rod steady and swing the line toward you. Catch hold of the fish with your other hand. Good job, you're a real angler now!

STAY SAFE! Try to hold the line above the fish so you don't get hurt by the sharp hook.

21

Handling Fish

You've got your fish! You now need to decide whether to keep it or release it back into the water. Either way, you will want to weigh and record it first. You'll need to act fast to be sure that the fish is unharmed.

Always be sure that your hands are wet when you pick up a fish. Otherwise you can remove some of the layer of slime that protects it. First, remove the hook from the fish's mouth. If you can see it, carefully turn it and slide it out. If it's deep inside the mouth, you'll need a special tool to remove it. If it's too deep to remove, cut the line and leave it in the fish. The hook will simply dissolve after a while.

Record your catch with a camera and the weighing scales.

Fish can take a few seconds to get used to being back in the water.

Take a photo of your fish for your records. To find the weight, attach the landing net with the fish inside it to your portable scales. You can weigh the empty net later, and subtract that number from your result to find the weight of the fish. You can measure your fish, too, and record it in your log book.

Try to cause the fish as little distress as possible. If you are returning it to the water, do it without delay. To let it recover from the shock of being caught, hold it gently underwater for a few seconds. When its **gills** are moving strongly, let it go.

STAY SAFE!

The fins and gills of a fish can be surprisingly sharp, so be careful when you handle it.

Cook It!

Part of the fun of fishing is eating what you've just caught. Check first that the rules of your fishing ground allow you to cook the fish on the land where you caught it.

It's great to cook your fish whole, but you need to remove the guts first. Ask an adult to help you do this because you'll need to use a sharp knife. Wash out the inside of the fish with cold water afterward. Don't worry about the scales. Once the fish is cooked, you'll remove the skin and the scales with it.

A lot of the fish's flavor is in the skin, so it's best to leave it on for cooking.

Fish Dish

Try this great recipe for
your fresh fish.

1 Clean the fish by gutting
and rinsing it.

2 In a bowl, combine the chopped
onion, lemon juice, herbs, salt,
and pepper.

3 Stuff each fish with some of
the herby onion mixture.

4 Wrap each fish in 1 or 2 bacon slices.

5 Wrap each fish in a piece of foil and
place on a hot grill over the fire for at
least 15 minutes. The cooking time
depends on the size of your fish.

6 Check that the flesh of the fish
is cooked through thoroughly.

7 Unwrap the cooked fish
and remove the skin.

You will need, for 4 people:

- 4 freshly-caught fish
- 1 medium onion, finely chopped
- 6–8 slices of bacon
- juice of 1 lemon
- rosemary, thyme, salt, and pepper
- foil

*Many people cook their fish
whole on a grill over an open fire.*

What's on the Line?

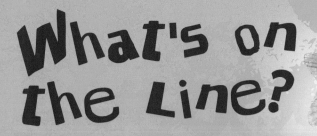

bluegill

The rivers, streams, and lakes of the United States are teeming with fish. With so many fish around, it's good to know what might end up on your line.

Fish that live in rivers, lakes, and streams are called freshwater fish because the water here is not salty. Some of the most popular freshwater fish for anglers are pike, walleye, catfish, bluegill, mahimahi, or dorado, and bass. There are many kinds of bass. The largemouth bass is the state fish of several southern states, although you'll find it in the north and west, too. This fish likes muddy, weedy water and is well known for putting up a good fight on the line! The smallmouth bass, which is also known as the bronzeback, swims in clear, rocky lakes.

smallmouth bass

catfish

crappie

Bluegills live in the shallow streams and rivers of the northeast. They like their water weedy and slow-moving. The walleye is more likely to be caught in the north, but the catfish swims in shallow waters throughout the United States. It has many nicknames, too, such as chucklehead, mudcat, and polliwog! Other fish you might find on the end of your line are muskellunge, yellow perch, crappie, and trout. There are dozens of varieties of darter fish and shiner fish, too. Get to know your fish and you'll soon be an expert angler.

largemouth bass

Go Green

We all have a responsibility to keep our wild places safe and unspoiled for the future. That way, everyone can continue to enjoy them. Wherever you are fishing, it's important to remember to respect the natural environment and make as little impact on it as you can.

Anglers need to be very aware of wildlife, because the gear they use can cause harm. Never leave tangles of line on the ground for birds and other animals to get caught up in. Hooks are dangerous, too. Don't leave them around with bait on, as they could tempt small creatures. Use barbless hooks because they cause less damage to the fish. Remember that other animals use the rivers and lakes, too. Bring in your line if there's a risk of birds swimming through it and getting snared.

Carefully pack up everything you brought with you.

After a perfect fishing trip, try to leave no trace behind.

The rules of clubs and landowners are there for a reason, so respect them. Don't catch more than you're allowed and release the fish if that's required. This preserves fish stocks for everyone.

When it's time to go, pack up everything, including your garbage, and take it home with you. The idea is to leave no trace behind!

Glossary

angling (ANG-gling) The sport of fishing.

bait (BAYT) Pieces of food put onto the hook to attract fish.

bale arm (BAYL AHRM) The lever on the reel that holds the line in place.

barb (BARB) A sharp spike.

bobber (BAHB-er) A small floating object that is attached to the line to catch fish near the surface.

cast (KAST) Using the rod to launch the line, hook, and bait into the water.

cinch knot (SINCH NOT) A knot used for tying the hook onto the line.

fly (FLY) An artificial insect made from feathers, fur, and wire used to attract fish.

freshwater (FRESH-wah-ter) Water that is not salty. Freshwater is found in rivers and lakes.

gills (GILZ) The slits on the side of a fish's body that it uses to breathe.

land (LAND) Bringing the fish out of the water.

license (LY-suns) A permit that allows you to fish in a location.

lures (LOORZ) Artificial small fish made from plastic, wood, or metal, used to attract fish.

reel (REEL) The device attached to the rod that controls the line.

rod (RAWD) The long pole that holds the fishing line.

sinker (SIN-ker) A weight used to take the hook and bait to the bottom of the water.

split shot (SPLIT SHOT) Small weights that can be squeezed onto the line.

spool (SPOOL) The part of the reel that holds the line.

strike (STRYK) When a sharp lift of the rod tip secures the hook in a fish's mouth.

tackle (TA-kul) All the equipment used for angling.

tackle box (TA-kul BOKS) A box with compartments for storing the hooks, flies, lures, line, and other equipment used for angling.

Further Reading

Howard, Melanie A. *Freshwater Fishing for Kids*. Into the Great Outdoors. Mankato, MN: Capstone Press, 2013.

Payment, Simone. *Bass Fishing*. Fishing: Tips & Techniques. New York: Rosen Central, 2012.

Schwartz, Tina P. *Fly-Fishing*. Reel It In. New York: PowerKids Press, 2012.

Websites

For web resources related to the subject of this book, go to: www.windmillbooks.com/weblinks and select this book's title.

Index